The Need for Contemplation

The Need for Contemplation

RENÉ VOILLAUME

translated by
ELIZABETH HAMILTON

Dimension Books · Denville, New Jersey

First American Edition
by Dimension Books Inc.

First published as
La Contemplation Aujourd'hui
in 1971 by
Les Editions du Cerf, Paris
This translation first published 1972 and
© *Darton, Longman & Todd Ltd, 1972*

ISBN 0 232 51181 0

Contents

6 CONTENTS

The Love of Jesus
and Prayer

To love God is to wait for someone

To love God might appear a very difficult thing. There
are even days when we doubt if it is possible. We are
only frail human beings. We cannot imagine love nor
is love within our power, unless, at least to some degree,
there is a sharing, a presence, evidence that comes
to us through the senses. How could there be love without
the presence of the beloved, without this sharing? Jesus
said: "He who loves me, does my will." And so we
wonder: "Does the love of Jesus amount, then, to no
more than this? All we are capable of feeling and doing,
does it mean merely to obey a law, to 'do' the Gospel?"
This, surely, is not at all our idea of love. We have the
impression that we are no longer concerned with our
feelings for a person, the person of God, the person of
Jesus – rather that we are confronted with a will made
known to us in the law of God and the law of the Gospel.
We know, of course, that, if we love someone, we cannot
do otherwise than comply fully not only with the will, but
also the inclinations, of that person. This is something
that follows from love. But, after all, should not the love
of God in our life be something different?

It is sometimes said that one of the signs of a genuine call to Christian perfection, one of the conditions for understanding this call and responding to it, is to have experienced God as a person. But what do we mean by this? We think of privileged moments when we have sensed a presence, a union. Doubtless we have all, at one time or another in our lives, gone through periods when this question did not arise: we knew for ourselves that to love Jesus was a reality which gladdened the heart, flooded us with joy, and we found in this union with God the fulness of our being. But this feeling passed. Then, there were somewhat disappointing times when we asked ourselves afresh: "What does loving God really mean?" Jesus, we are told, is a friend. How should this friendship show itself? How can we live it, grasp it, understand it, be certain of it here on earth? If we have given ourselves to him unconditionally in fidelity and chastity, in consecrated celibacy or in marriage, are we not entitled to expect that God will give us in return a love which, already in this world, brings some kind of fulfilment, some satisfaction to the yearnings of our hearts?

Besides, Jesus, it seems, promised this to his Apostles when the latter, through the mouth of Simon Peter, reminded him that they had left *all* to follow Him. Was it not for love they made this total renouncement? Saint Peter went on: "What, then, do we receive in return?" This is the reaction, we will say, of a love that was still selfish. Is there any need to expect something in return? If love is perfect, if it is total, should it not be unselfish, asking nothing in return? But doubtless the Apostles had not as yet reached this stage. And we ourselves, when we set out on the path of dispossession that Jesus showed to us ("Go, sell all that you have, deny yourself, take up your cross and follow me"), we, too, thought that we would enjoy in return a fulness of life. Our life as a Christian would be a journey in love, taking us from discovery to discovery, joy to joy, peace to peace, possession to possession. Yes, that, indeed, is what we thought.

In reality, there were days when we wondered if we had gone forward or backwards – whether, in fact, we still loved. We kept going on just because we had to go on. Granted, we did our duty, and with dedication, but were we waiting upon the Lord? When we love someone, we wait upon his will, we long to see him, to be at one with him. Instead, God seemed to be absent from our lives. When we were doing his will, obeying his law, it was rather as if we allowed ourselves to receive the stamp of his seal – but the surface, thus marked, showed no imprint. We dispossessed ourselves for his sake, yet still he was not ours. We made ourselves poor for his sake, to possess only him; yet it seemed that we could not possess him in this world. If we were living as religious, we had given up home, human love, and all the splendour, beauty, and fulfilment to which man is entitled. Even so, Jesus keeps us waiting. He is as good as absent from our lives. Yes, that is true : we do not yet possess him whom we love. And yet we do possess him!

We must, then, ask ourselves whether we are lacking

in hope. Are we eager – with all the eagerness of love – to enter that other life where Jesus will be given to us, where a new love will be able to flower? This other life eludes us, as we know too well. We cannot even find it desirable, since, while we are here on earth, we cannot imagine what such a life is like. What we have, what is familiar to us, this is what life here and now offers us. Such meagre satisfactions have at least the merit of being within our reach, adjusted to our human nature, to our senses, to man's heart that thirsts for joy, affection, and the presence of the one we love. This at least is something we understand, and to tear ourselves away is death indeed. And perhaps it is because we have no longer in our hearts a sufficiently lively expectation of eternity that we fall back on the transient, earthly facets of our Christian membership. We would like everything to be self-explanatory, to find fulfilment purely on the level of life in this world. We all of us shrink from death, feeling, instinctively, that it is the end of everything; whereas, viewed in the light of God's love, it can only be a beginning. God is eternal. Jesus was given to us not for a time only – we can possess him, enjoy his love in its fulness, only in life everlasting.

Meeting God in Christ

However, there were men and women who knew Jesus in the flesh, loved him, and followed him. The greatest commandment is to love God, Jesus said one day. And an apostle put this to him : "Lord, show us the Father and that is enough for us." We are familiar with the answer : "Have I been so long with you and you do not know me, Philip? He who has seen me has seen the Father." Jesus spoke of himself as the "way", as a point of departure. Further, to show the Apostles that he was truly the Word of God making manifest the Father, he had to leave them : "It is good for you that I go." Jesus, as man, reveals God and at the same time hides him. Such is our faith. We cannot cut ourselves off from Christ's humanity. And yet we must go beyond it. Nevertheless, Jesus, in his human nature, remains our "way". Through him we come to love God.

Read the gospels again, and see in them the different stages through which the Apostles passed as they came to know Jesus. They were won over by Jesus – they responded to his call as he sought out each of them individually. Consider how long it took them to recognize

the true face of Christ: this was to happen only on the
day when Saint Peter, in reply to a question put by Jesus,
acknowledged the divinity of Christ. After that, things
moved apace. The love felt by the Apostles was real: they
committed themselves to their Master in total fidelity,
boundless trust, despite their ignorance and their still all
too human reactions. They had changed very little during
those three years. Though they were in the company of
Jesus, they were the same men to whom the call from the
Lord had come. They were to participate in happenings
which they would not understand: the arrest of their
Master, his condemnation, Passion, crucifixion, and
death. After the Resurrection, consider what took place
between Jesus and the Apostles; the new call that came
to them on the shores of the lake, when Jesus, risen from
the dead, appeared to them once more. Consider how he
asks Peter – despite the latter's fall, indeed because of it –
to reaffirm his trust and his love: "Peter, do you love
me?"

And the Blessed Virgin, the Mother of Jesus? With a
mother's depth of insight she recognized God in her Son.
Open to the light of the Holy Spirit, she had a totally
luminous faith which enabled her to know that in him
was the Son of God. If she had not been enlightened by
the Spirit she would have seen Jesus as her son, only.
But, to her, he was more than a son.

Consider, too, the love of Mary Magdalene, the sinner.
She went to Jesus as she was. And she went to him as
man, but a man in whom she saw a prophet. And,

through an intuition that she herself did not clearly understand, she recognized in this prophet a cleansing power that came from God. She gave herself to Christ as she was, bringing her unguent, lavishing her attentions, kissing his feet. See her, distraught with grief, because Jesus was no longer there, in the tomb – because they have taken away his body. See her in the garden where the tomb was, searching for the body of Him whom she loved.

Moreover, in the Gospel there are many encounters between Jesus and those who seek him without being aware of it. There is the woman of Samaria. There is the woman taken in adultery. There is the penitent thief. Crucified at the side of Jesus, he recognized, when the Lord looked at him – in the radiance that shone from him even in the agony of his Passion – the mercy of God incarnate in a man.

All these encounters actually took place, in real life. Nevertheless, this kind of encounter with God – in the strict sense of the word – through the person of Christ, did not, in fact, come about in a human manner. It was at a level beyond the encounter itself, beyond attachment in the human sense of the word. The supernatural quality of man's encounter with God in Jesus is more obvious in our own times, for Christ is now in glory. He is, one may say, absent, in so far as he is man. His human nature, therefore, cannot in any way constitute an obstacle to our reaching beyond his humanity, in faith.

But these encounters with Jesus are not limited to the

years of his life on earth. The history of the saints in the Church, the history of all men and women who have loved the Lord, show us this clearly. These, one and all, encountered him. There is, then, in every Christian, deep in the soul, a supernatural awareness, implanted by grace, which makes possible such an encounter with God.

The bride in the Song of Songs

We sometimes wonder what the love of Jesus can mean. We ask ourselves if we should dismiss conceptions which are over-emotional or which, closely associated with the senses, denote a mere fleeting awareness of the supernatural. On the contrary, such moments as these show the reality of this love – a love which has roots in us, grows, and, at times, takes entire possession of us. A gift from God, this love is also our work. It is for us to tend its seed, to see that the roots strike deep, even if we cannot make it mature to the point of our being able to enjoy and partake of its fruits. Yes, if we want to do so, we can love the Lord because he has first loved us, and because he has called us, and because we have left all to follow him. And we must not undervalue the fact of our having "left all", as if we had "left all" for nothing. To do so, would be to narrow the horizons of our earthly life, to shrivel up into ourselves, while continuing to live in a state of detachment from the world, perhaps a little regretfully – trying to fill, somehow or other, the emptiness of our lives because we have not found him for whom we left all. What matters is that there should be no question of our hankering after what we have left. For, in reality, we have found him for whom we were searching.

There is a book which is not always very easy to understand, and which gives scandal to some people : the Song of Songs. Some see it as an erotic poem, others as a song about profane love. In fact, it is an inspired book, included among the canonical books of the Old Testament to show us beyond all doubt that the love of God is a genuine love : a reality on a lofty plane. The love of God surpasses all imaginable human love, yet it is, if I may say so, of the same stuff. For it is in human love that God has found the most fitting imagery in which to convey the nature of the love that one day will flower in all its fulness between him and ourselves. That is the meaning of the Song of Songs. The book has to be read several times, with eyes that can look face to face at the reality of the love revealed in the heart of Christ. In this mysterious book we have the story of our relations with Jesus : the story of a soul in search of a God who is Love. Why not have such a goal? Why be content with less? Christians, you have chosen to give your life to Love : to the love of God, once and for all, unconditionally. The Lord has called you, as he has called the bride in the Song of Songs. Not that it would be right to become lost in dreams and illusions that are the fruit of the imagination. We should, nevertheless, believe to the point of surrendering our entire life to a Love that is unlike any other. If Christianity has a witness to give to the world, it is to show that, in choosing to follow Christ, we have chosen to surrender ourselves to this Love, and that this same Love so stamps our behaviour that men of good will can have at least an inkling that it is this which actuates our lives.

To know God

I must now call to mind the supernatural truths which are the foundation of this life of prayer, and show that prayer is an imperative, if one is to love Christ.

There is no love without knowledge, that is obvious. How can one love a person whom one does not know? There is no love without a presence: one cannot love someone who is for ever at a distance. There is no love without sharing, for friendship – and this is the most perfect form of love – presupposes a response. Finally, there is no love which does not look forward to a union that, as time goes on, will become more and more complete and, finally, eternal. Indeed, there is no love worthy of the name which has not the wish for eternity. I shall now take up each of these requisites of love, showing how they lead, quite naturally, to a life of prayer.

How can we encounter God and know him well enough to be able to love him? How can we find the Lord, we who are living now? As to this, I do not see much difference between our situation today and that of the early Christians who, without having themselves seen the Saviour, had received the testimony of the Apostles.

Besides, we must remind ourselves that we will not come
to know Jesus merely by gathering together the evidence
provided by those who saw him and who record for us in
the gospels all he did and said, thus disclosing his personality, his teachings, the manifestations of his love, the
unfolding of his Passion. Of course, we must first of all
know Jesus in his human nature. He came to us by this
way, and it is on this way we shall meet him. That is
why the Gospel is indispensable as a basis of our knowledge of Jesus, and therefore the foundation of our love
for him.

But this kind of knowledge, in isolation, would be quite
inadequate. Even when Jesus was on earth it was not
enough to see him and to hear him. To be won over by
him, to believe in him, to recognize him as God, there
had to be openness of heart, a child's readiness to be
taught, and the grace of the Holy Spirit. Now, grace to
encounter God in Jesus was not given to all who were in
the company of the Lord. Equally, grace to encounter
the Lord is not given to everyone who reads the Gospel.
The attitude of mind that was called for during Christ's
life on earth is necessary, if, while we read, we are to
recognize Jesus as the Son of God, our Saviour, and the
sole object of our love.

To be able to know God is not, then, something that
comes from ourselves. Jesus himself often said this. The
grace of enlightenment and knowledge, implanted in our
hearts, is a fruit of our faith given to us through baptism.
It imparts an awareness of our dependence on God as

our Father, enabling us, without our understanding how this is so, to penetrate into his mystery. This awareness, which makes it possible for us to know God as our Father, comes from a permanent disposition, which is none other than the grace of faith, and which enables us to be enlightened at every moment by the gifts of the Holy Spirit. Obviously it is not in a permanent manner that we are granted the enlightenment of God's presence, nor does it happen every day. This is one of the mysteries of God's love: it is very hard to explain. Only those who have experienced the love of Jesus can understand how it can grow, strike roots, reveal itself through insights that are not of the order of the senses, but beyond this and incomparably more profound. These insights give us light and strength. They also give us certainty. It is knowledge of this kind which enables us to live the Gospel and allows us to align ourselves once and for all with Jesus Christ.

So much, then, for the first requisite of prayer. But we cannot attain to this intimate knowledge of God without times given to silent reflection in mental prayer. In our active life, in devoting ourselves to the service of others, in carrying out in a spirit of generosity the obligations of our calling, we receive, provided we listen to the promptings of love, the grace of union with Christ. But the grace of light and of knowledge, which is at the root of this intimate love and this friendship which binds us to Jesus, is normally received only during the silence of mental prayer: in those moments which we devote solely

to Jesus because we want to be with him as a person, as a
friend. Whenever we withdraw into solitude and silence
to find him and him alone, we are, by this very fact,
making him an offering of ourselves. To refuse or to
neglect to do so would amount to ignoring him as a
person. Could we love a friend deeply without feeling a
need to meet him from time to time, simply to be with
him, to enjoy one another's company, to get to know him
better, to tell him of our love? There must be, then, in
the life of every Christian, and especially in that of every
religious, a minimum of what I would call contemplative
prayer: that is to say, prayer which is wholly directed
towards the knowledge of the Beloved – thirsting for that
knowledge in the light of the Spirit. There is a form of
prayer, therefore, which is a search for the knowledge of
God in the Holy Spirit. It is during this prayer that we
are granted an awareness of God in our heart and soul.
There are scarcely any of us who have not at one time or
another realized what such moments mean. If it is not in
our power to experience these through our own efforts, it
is at least in our power to wish for them, to ask for them,
and, through persevering generously in prayer, to be in
readiness to receive them.

God's presence at the root of our being

It is not enough to know God through the intellect. We desire, we long, that he whom we love should be with us. In fact, God is with us : Jesus is with us. In the first place, in the depths of our being (we seldom think of this), at our very roots, there is a presence : that of the Trinity and the Word of God through whom all things were made. The roots of our personality, the roots of our being, plunge deep into the creative act of the Word. We hardly ever ask ourselves how it comes about that we have being, that we exist – we ourselves, not someone else – at this moment of history and in this particular place. This kind of question can make our heads spin. Countless human beings have lived, generations without number have followed one upon another down the centuries and will continue to do so after I have gone. And here I am, now, in existence. A precise number of years ago I was born and I travel towards my death. We are aware of this : the fact of our existence means that something unique was done to bring us into being.

Could we really be content to be no more than the product of an evolution that has continued down the centuries, originating from the first cells? Whatever may be the advances of science, to whatever degree of perfection, in the field of scientific discovery, life may evolve, the fact will always remain that a human "person" can only come into being through the intervention of the creative word of God. Science will never be able to prove otherwise. Nor, on the other hand, will it be able to prove the existence of the creative act.

As we all know, we each are a reality apart, unlike any other in the world. We exist because the Word has spoken the name of each one of us. And because this is so, we have come into being, having in our hearts a spark of infinity – a longing for life, a longing for love, a longing for eternity. Let us not quench such a feeling. On the contrary, we should strive to grasp its meaning, in moments of silent reflection – for it is at such times that we begin to worship God, our Creator. Here is the well-spring of the love of him who, in giving us life, has given us all. If we cut ourselves off from this source of life and being, if we no longer have within us this immeasurable longing for life, we shall withdraw into ourselves, imprison ourselves within the frustrations and anguish of the present life – so that, sometimes, we shall no longer have the will to live. Thus, man can bring upon himself his own destruction. At times we lose our footing on this precarious slope, whereas, if we reflected how the roots of our being go deep into the Word spoken by him who created us, we would feel stirring within a disposition which is none other than adoration, praise of God, and thanksgiving for the gift of life bestowed upon us.

The presence of Christ our Saviour

But there is even more. God has given us a life higher
than our human life : the life of the children of God, in
Christ, through his grace. Moreover, if we are able to
grasp, through a supernatural insight, our total dependence on the Word who created us, this is because we have
in us, as I have said, an awareness that God is our Father.
The Trinity dwells within us, we within the Trinity.
Jesus said : "We will come and make our abode in them."
This is the presence of grace. Now, all prayer is the
expression, the vital act, of this life which, in us, is faith,
love, and hope. When these gifts, which direct us towards
God, find expression, are translated into action, we are
praying.

There is in us yet another presence of Jesus : the
presence of his blood. I deliberately say "his blood" : the
blood that has redeemed us. For once we begin to realize
the meaning of life in God, our problem is that of sin,
infidelity – in a word, anything that can keep us apart
from God. The further on we go, the more we are aware
that there is, deep within us, a wretchedness that is a
source of profound discouragement – in which are rooted

all possible ills. And indeed we sin. Yet we know, we believe with all the strength of our faith, that we have been redeemed by the blood of Jesus Christ. Consider the bonds uniting Mary Magdalene to Jesus. They are the bonds of forgiveness. Mary Magdalene has been forgiven, cleansed by the blood of Jesus. So has the woman of Samaria. And the woman taken in adultery. And the thief who died at his side.

And so another prayer should well up in our soul: the basic prayer of petition. Of course we know how to ask for the many things we want for our life from day to day. And we are entitled to do so. But there is a different prayer of petition, which goes to the heart of the matter. In the prayer which Jesus teaches us, the Our Father, he restricts himself to essentials: the kingdom of God, our daily bread, the forgiveness of sins. It is, indeed, the great prayer. Certainly, man should do all in his power to assume responsibility for the affairs of this world. Moreover, he should also recognize the autonomy of the temporal order, fully legitimate in its own sphere. But this makes all the more real, all the more tragic, the drama which has its origin in man's weakness in exercising his freedom: this mystery of evil which shows itself in the heart of every human being. We have only to see the evils of all kinds, the disasters, which man can set in train. Furthermore, if it is our duty to work with all our might in the field of politics, sociology, and education, there is, we are well aware, a limit beyond which man, despite all his efforts, all his objectives, cannot go. It is the limit set to these activities by human freedom and the flaws inherent in it. Here, I would suggest, is the real field for the prayer of supplication and intercession. Here, we see unfold the conflict, on which all else depends, between God's grace and man's freedom. Here, beyond question, is the need for prayer.

And we are confronted with this problem in ourselves. Can we escape from this slavery of sin? Can we escape from our weaknesses, our wretchedness, our bondage, if we do not pray, if we do not implore the Lord to heal us? We know very well that, left alone, we cannot save ourselves. We must accept the fact that we are sinners in need of forgiveness. One would like to be a saint, having no need of forgiveness, but this is a fatal delusion. Sometimes we even worsen our condition by efforts of the will, which create tension to no purpose. We would rather not be sinners, whereas the attitude which would really set us free would be to learn to accept forgiveness. Consider Mary Magdalene, the public sinner. If we love God, we must beg the Lord to "deliver us from evil and lead us not into temptation".

There is yet another presence of Jesus in the Church and it affects every one of us: it is the presence of the prayer of Christ. All that we are, all the good that is ours, all that we receive in the way of grace – all this has been won for us through the prayer of Christ. The Church itself is the fruit of Christ's prayer. The charisms which have been bestowed on the Church are also the fruits of Christ's prayer. "I have prayed", Jesus said to Peter, "that your faith may not fail." Christ prayed before he chose his Apostles. We, too, are the object of the prayer of Christ. This prayer enfolds us. It is a true presence of Christ in our lives. We are sheltered by the prayer of Christ who makes unceasing intercession before the Father.

But we, as his followers – here we have another reason for praying – are in duty bound to unite ourselves to this prayer of Christ. This participation in his intercession, this need to "pray without ceasing", has been in evidence in the Church from earliest times. To come nearer our own day, this is one of the purposes of prolonged prayer of adoration before the Blessed Sacrament. The Euchar-ist, because it is the presence of the living Christ, not only re-enacts the sacrifice of Christ, it contains his unceasing prayer and provides us with an outward sign of this reality.

The part played by man

As I have already said, to share in a spirit of friendship is an essential quality in love. God gives to us. Can we, in our turn, give something to God? If we can give nothing, can we speak of real love between friends? Here, we are confronted with the mystery of man's creation. God willed that man should be free. And because man is free, he can choose, he can commit himself, he can give. Because he is free, he can love and he can refuse to love. Yet he would not be able to give anything at all, if he did not first receive from God what it is he should give. Here, indeed, is the wondrous mystery of man's creation in the image of God, which he carries within him and of which we must take account. Above all, this image of God is the life of grace in us: a sharing in the life of the Trinity concealed under a created form, adapted to our human nature.

This life of the Trinity which, in the first place, comes down to us through Christ – that is, Christ in his humanity – and, from Christ, has overflowed into us, permeates the members of the body of which he is the head. This same life is itself a sharing which is beyond human understanding. God allows us to share in his life. He gives us redemption. He gives us his love. He gives us the grace which enables us to live our life on earth in a growth towards perfection. But he does not treat us as beings who have no freedom : in all things he asks for our responsible co-operation. This is where the sharing comes in. Yes, we can give our life to Jesus; we can give him our freedom : we can associate ourselves with him in his sacrifice on the cross. But why should Jesus alone, once and for all, have consummated in suffering this sacrifice which saves the world? Is nothing asked of us other than to profit from this – to present ourselves merely as the recipients of the graces of the Resurrection, without previously having had to share in the mystery of his death and Passion? This would be too easy. Through baptism we are dead with Christ and risen with him. Yes, we are dead with Christ, and this death of the Saviour operates in us as long as we are in our present state of transition, movement, and growth in perfection, which is how it is here on earth.

We can also give to Jesus our freedom, wholly and irrevocably, and, through the exercise of this freedom, consecrate to him our entire life – and this is what being a religious means. We can, in freedom and motivated by love, offer him our crosses or, to be precise, offer him our sufferings and difficulties, that these may become crosses. For the word "cross" has been all too often used carelessly to mean any suffering. Every suffering is not necessarily a cross. To become one, suffering must be offered to God with the intention of our participating in the work of redemption, sharing in the cross of Jesus. Here we touch on a mystery : the mystery of evil in the world. There are sufferings that, far from being crosses which save, are weights which crush. There are sufferings which break us, and cause us revulsion. These are an evil, a scandal, no less than sin. Christians, in that they have knowledge of the Passion of Christ and are born again through this Passion, have a duty to transmute suffering into a cross of redemption – our sufferings and those of the rest of mankind, offering these to God in a prayer of supplication. For only the Lord, who alone is our Saviour, can transmute into a cross of salvation the suffering of man that is in itself futile and repellent. But we are bound one to another. Not even the work of Christ can be effective if it does not function through the freedom of man. It cannot be repeated too often that every concept of the redemption and regeneration of human nature through grace is at fault if it does not take into account the need for man's co-operation. That is why we must not fail to work resolutely with Jesus.

upon death, this, without any doubt, is, for each one of us, very close. The expectation of this encounter, so near to us, should have a place in our prayer: it should make our prayer well up.

My intention has been to establish the basis of prayer, which is, in fact, the grace bestowed upon us in virtue of our adoption as the children of God. To pray is to be like a child who needs his father and shows to him his confidence and love. Prayer is the manifestation of a life which has been given to us. This life needs to grow, to expand. For the time being it is at the stage when it has to gain strength in the darkness of faith. It cannot yet expand in all its fulness. And this vital power ought to find expression in prayer, in a dialogue with God and with Jesus.

Contemplation in the Church Today

spontaneous impulse, in this sharing of life which united the Apostles to Jesus, we have in embryo the entire contemplative life of the Church. Indeed, ever since this experience of the Apostles, the contemplation of the God of truth, life, and love, revealed in Christ, has been accepted as something essential to the full flowering of the Christian life.

In the light and in the wake of this experience of the Apostles, followed by that of Saint Paul and the early

I go to prepare a home for you I shall come back to take you with me, that where I am you may be also." (Jn. 14. 2.)

"I wish that where I am they also may be with me, that they may see my glory which you have bestowed on me." (Jn. 17. 24.).

"Truly, I say to you, today you will be with me in paradise." (Lk. 23. 42.)

And there is the witness given by Saint Paul: "Our home is in heaven. It is to heaven that we look expectantly for the coming of our Lord and Saviour Jesus Christ; He will form this humbled body of ours anew, moulding it into the image of his glorified body, so effective is his power to make all things new." (Ph. 3. 20–21.).

"If indeed we believe that Jesus died and rose again, so it will be for those who have died in Jesus; God will unite these again to Him . . . And thus we will be for ever with the Lord." (1. Th. 4. 14–18.)

"If from human motives I have fought against beasts at Ephesus, what has it availed me? If the dead do not rise again, let us eat and drink, for tomorrow we shall die." (1. Cor. 15. 32–33.)

"We know that he who raised the Lord Jesus from the dead will raise us, too, with Jesus, and bring us, together with you, into his presence." (2. Cor. 4. 14.)

"We have this anchorage for our souls, sure and immovable – reaching into the inner sanctuary beyond the veil, where Jesus, who goes before us, has already entered." (He. 6. 19.)

disciples, countless persons from the first century on –
some in the desert, some through associating themselves
with Christ in the supreme sacrifice of martyrdom –
have borne witness, in their search for God, to the
dynamic character of this aspect (I would call it the
ultimate purpose) of the Christian life, which constitutes
nothing else than a desire to be with Christ for ever. For
these witnesses are convinced that the true destiny of
every human being is to be found in a fulness of union,
in vision and love, in the life of Christ in eternity. The
entire evolution of the religious life in the Church should
be recalled at this point, along with the great contemplatives who mark out the way, from Antony the
Hermit, Pacomius, and Benedict to Father de Foucauld :
all of them shining examples whose lives are moulded to
the pattern of Christ, all of them consumed with a longing to be with him hereafter, not seeking to escape from
the world, but obeying the imperative of love and
attaining to the fulness of truth.

Opinions have varied, of course, down the centuries as
to the meaning of holiness and the paths that lead to it –
the self-denial and purgation that it demands, the
different kinds of bodily and spiritual asceticism thought
of as necessary conditions for contemplative prayer.
Moreover, the different approaches to contemplation
itself have a relative character. They reflect, too, something of the philosophical, psychological, or theological
attitudes of an epoch. Yet, the relative character of these
practices, which were not immune from imperfections or

abuses, should not allow us to forget the overriding authenticity of the supernatural contemplative states which accompanied them and to which they gave expression, even though they did so in a clumsy manner. It is natural that the ways and means employed to express the contemplative state should be influenced by the evolution of the spiritual life of the Church – and enriched, furthermore, by the experience of the greatest saints.

As to the authenticity of the contemplative experience in the Church, this experience presents itself to us as a fact. And this is all-important. The trappings that go with it can always be questionable. False mystics can always be subject to delusion. No one, however, could seriously put in doubt the over-all authenticity of so many experiences of a supernatural union with God.

Contemplation was lived before it was called by this name. It was only gradually, as the theology of spirituality was formulated, that the concept of this kind of prayer emerged, while at the same time the idea of a contemplative life in religion was taking a more definite shape and its value and role in the Church were being assessed. Contemplatives called upon to encourage others to follow in their path were led to reflect upon their personal experience. And they tried to put this in words, to be able to share it. Moreover, they had to suggest the means that seemed to them most appropriate for fostering the birth and growth of an authentic contemplative prayer.

Some have found fault with the use of the word contemplation. They have even denied to the reality so named a specifically Christian value. Such critics have seen underlying it a concept of the universe peculiar to a debatable philosophical view that goes back beyond Christianity. One must, indeed, acknowledge the influences that, in the course of the Church's life, have left their mark on the language through which the masters of spirituality have tried to record their experiences. And here we touch on the more general problem as to how to give expression to Christian doctrine. And we know, today, the importance of this, and the difficulty involved. Here I shall merely remark that the theology of the contemplative life must, above all, take into account an existential fact, or, to be precise, a number of actual experiences – experiences which this same theology is required to clarify in the light of a theology of grace and of the relationship possible on a supernatural plane between a Christian and God, in the persons of the Trinity, as revealed in Christ. Besides, even if the word contemplation is not Christian in origin, it has assumed in theological language a precise meaning, denoting a reality which remains basically unchanged through the history of spirituality. We would do well to translate this reality into intelligible terms. Indeed, it is vital that we be able to reflect upon such a reality at the present time.

An element essential to every Christian life

Before going further we must define briefly what is meant
by contemplation in the Christian sense of the word. We
are concerned here with a reality which touches the life
of a human being at its deepest level : one which assumes
that a relationship of knowledge and friendship can be
established between man and a God who reveals himself
as a personal being. It follows, therefore, that the meaning we attach to such a state and the value we give it
depends on our conception of the human intelligence and
its capacity for true knowledge. If we accept contemplation in the Church as a supernatural reality concerning
which we can have no doubts, we must understand what
the statement of this fact implies. Indeed, we have to
grant a number of premises without which contemplation would be meaningless or a mere subjective illusion.
These premises are either realities to which faith alone
can attain or a number of affirmations of a philosophical
order which are basically founded on common sense. I
will touch on these premises, briefly.

If contemplation is to be possible, it follows, in the first
place, not only that God, in the Three Persons of the

Trinity, revealed in Christ, must subsist in himself as a supreme reality distinct from the created universe, but also that man, in his capacity to know and love what is highest, can be raised up to participate in a true union in the fulness of the life of God. Further, it means that such a union is in line with the greatest perfection to which man can aspire (and indeed far beyond), as a fulness of life in accordance with intelligence and love. In a word, contemplation, to have meaning, presupposes that man is made for God : that only in him can be found that perfect, eternal fulfilment which we call the beatific vision : the ultimate fruit of Redemption won through Christ.

All the great Christian contemplatives are at one in their witness. Whatever their spiritual road, union with God is seen as real – as having a reality more deeply imbedded in experience, more surely established, more firmly rooted in being and certainty, than any experience known in the material world. In this sense, it is true to say that the contemplatives are, of all men, the most realistic.

They reveal, too, out of their experience, to what degree this apprehension of the God who is Truth – an apprehension which no words can describe, which is totally luminous yet mysteriously dark – is the fruit of a great love and at the same time functions within this love; that, furthermore, such a knowledge of God brings in its turn an increase of love. The intimate union with his God, into which the Christian can be brought by

Christ, is, in the last analysis, a union of love, but a love which cannot exist without at least some knowledge of the splendour, the beauty, and the truth of God – in a word, all that makes him whom we love worthy of being loved. How could a God, who is unknowable, be truly loved? How could an impersonal God, in whom I could not find satisfaction for the overriding demands of my mind and my heart – how could such a God be my Beloved? How could a God who is not at the same time the well-spring of my life and he who one day will be its fulfilment in eternity – how, I ask, could he win me, how could he have the right to take captive my life and my love?

But, it will be objected, are not these contemplatives men apart? What common ground can exist between their experience, granted it is genuine, and the Christian life as it has been presented to Christians as a whole, and even to those whom the Lord has called to the work of the apostolate? True, just as all are not called to the charism of the apostolate, so all are not called in the same degree to union with God through contemplation. Nevertheless, just as every Christian is invited through Baptism to participate in the apostolate of the Church, in accordance with his calling and potentialities, so, too, every Christian is invited in this world to at least a minimum of knowledge and love of God, in the light of the gifts bestowed by the Holy Spirit, without which he would be unable to pray, love the Lord, and live by the Gospel. This fundamental unity in the Christian life,

which underlies its diverse functions and charisms, has
assumed a new importance in recent times. All possess
the same life, with its basic elements, though all are not
called upon to develop these in the same way. This union
of knowledge and love which we call contemplation –
whether it is gradually developed or suddenly bestowed
– must be, it appears, one of the elements essential to
every Christian life. If, therefore, in every Christian there
must be at least a seed of contemplation, it is desirable
that this seed should grow to the fullest possible extent,
in proportion to a person's generosity and charity. Moreover, this seed implanted in the heart of a follower of
Christ cannot be allowed to shrivel without serious
damage to the integrity and the perfection of his Christian life.

This by no means implies that all Christians are called
upon to dedicate their lives, in actual fact, to the attainment of a measure of fulfilment in the contemplative life.
This would require, normally, conditions of silence and
prayer which are not granted to all. However, the evolution of spirituality in the Church, as also in the religious
life, seems to move steadily towards a more and more
widespread diffusion of spiritual values which at the
beginning were the prerogative of a few. Thus, after
appearing to be reserved, in general, for monks, then
religious or clergy, the attainment of some degree of
union with the Lord through the practice of mental
prayer was later presented as an ideal within the reach of
all fervent Christians, whatever their estate. With the

mendicant Orders the religious life came out of the cloister, and, with Saint Ignatius, infiltrated the work of the apostolate. Then, again, the birth of Third Orders put evangelical perfection within the reach of the laity, and Saint Francis de Sales showed that it was possible for sincere Christians, immersed in the world, to practise mental prayer and experience intimate union with God. We shall see, presently, how Father de Foucauld, by his life and his foundations, takes his place in the same tradition in the evolution of spirituality.

False dilemmas

But, it will be objected, what I have just said about the value of contemplation is surely bound up with an individualistic concept of personal salvation that is now outdated? Are we not inclined, today, to dismiss as waste of time the inactivity of the contemplatives who cut themselves off from the affairs of the world at the very time when these latter present themselves more and more as having the first claim on man's attention? Only the service of others, it is said, can foster a charity that is without self-deception. In short, the contemplative life is alleged to be a relic of an outdated stage in the evolution of religion.

It is essential, in view of the objections raised against this life of contemplation, to examine, without trying to avoid the issues, a number of basic questions inevitably posed by the world as it is today. These are the positive value of this world versus life eternal; the concept of collective salvation through the establishment of the kingdom of God on earth versus personal salvation in the vision of God; mass social and cultural development seen as an irreversible trend in the evolution of the

society of tomorrow versus the affirmation of the importance of each man's personal destiny; finally, the full
responsibility of man in the struggle against evil, versus
the redemptive value of Christ's suffering on the cross.

Now, contemplatives, by the mere fact of their existence, compel us to face these problems. Moreover, the
contradictions that I have just listed have never been felt
more keenly. Man, it seems, is not yet able to accept that
he is powerless to measure the mysterious depth of his
own nature. Still less has he succeeded in recognizing
that he cannot, by his own efforts, fill the void that is
within him. Too often he wants to solve his problems in
terms of options, exclusive choices. Confronted, as it
were, with a road that forks in two directions, he cannot
take one way without abandoning the other. One leads
to the recognition of the world as having a quasi-
absolute value, the first task encumbent upon man being,
then, to work for its construction, with the purpose of
establishing the kingdom of God here on earth, in justice
and in peace. The other is the way of detachment from
things created, because they are transitory; attachment
to the true values of eternity, in poverty of spirit, in the
hope of personal salvation, in the vision of God who
alone is able to satisfy the yearning of man's heart –
human nature being delivered from evil and death
through the Resurrection of Christ.

Why limit ourselves to an exclusive choice? Why set
these two concepts one against the other? The sole solution is to accept the contrasting aspects inherent in this

double reality: visible and invisible; present and future; temporal and eternal – to face courageously the mystery of man's destiny in all its reality, with the terrifying demands it brings, the tensions, the continuous straining to outreach oneself. Must not man become resigned, in humility, to the fact that, if he confronts his destiny alone, he cannot escape his predicament, because the ideal to which he is called is something beyond his reach. When seeking a solution for our problems, we have difficulty in coming to terms with this shadow of transcendence, this baffling mystery which we find in ourselves and which, in every human being, is the mark of God. Yet, in this direction alone can we hope to be able to reconcile what appears to be irreconcilable.

The difficulty comes, then, not from the facts in themselves which constitute the reality of the world nor from the situations to which men are exposed. It arises because these realities and these situations are no longer perceived face to face, objectively, but as already interpreted in the light of a particular concept of man, his history, and his evolution on earth – a concept depending on a particular philosophical view of the universe which is not the only one able to take account of these facts. We no longer know how to look face to face – I was going to say with simplicity – at reality, since, in general, we are unaware that what we are accepting as facts beyond dispute are actually facts already interpreted. The paradox that appears to oppose this world to the world of faith derives from a contradiction between two concepts of the universe, rather than between two realities that are equally true.

The concept of the universe based on dialectic materialism, one that is prevalent today, is far from being, then, the only one that can take into account the meaning of history and the achievements of the modern world. In so far as the distinction is not made between the real and the interpretation of the real, the difficulty of reconciling the world of faith and that of man will remain. Christians will continue to be caught in this dilemma. Either they will appear to be strangers in the world, unable to accept its tasks without reservation, or they will have to deny the authenticity of their faith, while yielding to the temptation to rethink its formulation, if not its content, in the light of concepts of the world and the universe, all of which reflect a materialistic viewpoint. The contemplatives are incapable of this divided thinking. And in this lies their strength.

To know man in all his dimensions

I would like to give some more concrete examples of what I have just put forward.

For the first time in his history man finds himself at one and the same time fully responsible for his destiny on earth and aware of having at his disposal the means of realizing this. Moreover, he claims that he can do so in complete freedom. This awakening to an awareness of his responsibility in relation to his destiny is a matter of the utmost importance to man. But it brings serious obligations, since the interpretation to be put upon this destiny, and the nature of the means to be used to realize it, remain a matter of his choice. When, in making this choice, man declares that he is totally free from every law or every reality superior to himself, we are no longer concerned simply with facts, but with an interpretation of these facts.

When we accept too readily the use of the word irreversibility to describe particular phenomena in the social or economic evolution – as if man were the plaything of a blind, compelling force – or when we speak of total secularization and desacralization as an inevitable and definitive phase in human society, we are not stating particular sociological facts, we are interpreting them. Actually, a Christian who is true to the lights of his faith would have nothing more to do or say in a world thus interpreted, whereas he has no difficulty in looking at the realities of this world and interpreting them in a manner no less valid, by setting these in the light of realities contemplated by him in the invisible world. The more man wants to be responsible for himself, the more, unless he is to destroy himself, he will have to realize that he is bound to live in conformity with the divine and human realities which shape his true destiny.

The acceptance, without reservation, of the tasks required for the organization of the earthly city is, indeed, a challenge – one that the past has never known – calling for the realization of love in accordance with wholly new dimensions and bringing into play complex means. To love man means to desire his good and to be ready to lay down one's life to attain this for him. Now, to determine the nature of this good presupposes a knowledge of man in all his dimensions, even when these reach into eternity. The man of faith, whose vision has been refined by familiarity with the mystery of God, is, more than any other, fitted to understand man in his totality and so to love him in truth. And this involves consequences even for the building of the earthly city. The hope which goes beyond this world, far from weakening the zeal to build this city, is, by a strange paradox, indispensable. In short, man is incapable of bringing to the building of his own city the spirit which alone can make it fully human, if he does not direct his gaze beyond time to the city which is eternal. Unless he looks to this eternal city, the city here on earth becomes uninhabitable. Every human being has within him, however much or little he may be aware of it, a contemplative dimension which he cannot deny unless he is to consign himself to unhappiness and, probably, despair. In the world of men, the contemplatives are the privileged witnesses of this dimension.

Another characteristic often emphasized in the world today is a process whereby the individual is more and more submerged into the mass – "massification", to use modern jargon – and this confronts us sharply with the problem of personal fulfilment. Here, again, the contemplative knows from experience that only in God can man find his complete fulfilment. He does not deny, of course, that, to realize himself fully on earth, man must receive from his brothers and give to them in his turn, through mutual cultural exchanges, which nothing else can replace, all those things which society alone can provide. But he knows also that, to whatever heights of fraternity and justice it may rise, this human society cannot satisfy man's aspirations.

There is in the world another reality in which the contemplative participates at a deeper level than anyone else. And this is the suffering which, under its many names, assails man in mind, heart, and body.

Modern man's confidence that he can free himself, by his own efforts, from all the forms of servitude of which he is the victim, fosters sometimes a kind of triumphalism, and makes him lose his sense of reality as to the place of suffering in our lives. The contemplative, because he has descended with Christ crucified into the depths of the mystery of human suffering, is better able than anyone else to shower tenderness on those who are stricken down by misfortune. Whatever be the efforts made by man to eradicate suffering from the world, the cross of Christ will always remain the sole reality which can hold back, when on the brink of despair or filled with revulsion in the face of the meaninglessness of life, those for whom, broken or crushed by suffering, no solace offered by man can suffice. Not all the ideologies, not all the efforts of man, can remove the need for, nor the value of, the cross of Christ. Only if we contemplate the cross can we enter into the full meaning of union with God in the redemption. Moreover, it is this same love, crucified, which will labour, with the greatest determination and to the greatest advantage, to banish suffering, and yet not cease to confer upon the same suffering a redemptive power that comes from God.

Many persons, Christians and non-Christians, whose thought has been influenced by a particular philosophy and by modern scientific attitudes, profess themselves no longer able to admit the concept of God as presented by the Church. Any facet of the human personality that has been projected upon this concept, must, they feel, be stripped away. They go so far as to speak of idols. Others even maintain that we can neither say anything nor can we know anything about God. Now in so far as this demand to clarify and advance in the knowledge of God is legitimate and possible, it must be recognized that the contemplatives, who have been able to translate their experience of the divine into human language, give us the loftiest and the purest possible concept of God. To appreciate this, we have only to read the greatest among them – Saint John of the Cross, for example. It is not that we are unable to know God with the intelligence – we cannot adequately express his mystery, which is a different thing. The language of the mystics cannot, of course, match that of science or reason. Yet, in a world craving for evidence from real life, it will remain one of the means through which our contemporaries can find God.

Lastly, in an affluent society and in the face of progress that too often is translated solely in terms of economics, we would do well to reflect that it is increasingly difficult to see in poverty anything other than an evil to be uprooted. Caught in the present current of euphoria, even religious reach the point of asking themselves whether renouncement of the good things of this world, as suggested by Christ, should not be replaced by what could be described as the co-existence of a certain self-denial combined with a positive acceptance of the world. Now, only the contemplation of the eternal values that belong to the kingdom of God, and the expectation of attaining to these, can make sense of poverty as presented to us in the Gospel. Christ himself, in his teaching, always set the renunciation of the things which pass away over against the possession of those which are abiding.

Furthermore, it is relevant to point out that in proportion as a religious ceases to direct his life by means of contemplation towards a total union with Christ, he is no longer able to understand the value to be put upon his consecrated celibacy, or to fulfil its demands in a spirit of peace and joy founded on hope – seeing it as a gift fruitful to the Church.

Recently in a common pronouncement, the major Superiors in Holland wrote :

"The purpose of consecrated celibacy goes deeper. It must be sought in a personal experience of God. According to the Gospels one cannot choose celibacy and remain faithful to it, unless in one way or another, however feebly, one has the conviction, founded upon experience, that God gives himself to man in love, and that to remain celibate is something worthwhile. . . . In a world in which faith is questioned, we should not be surprised to find a crisis in both prayer and celibacy. Prayer and continence are related : in one case as in the other, it is a matter of waiting upon the will of him who has revealed himself not only to this world but to ourselves. Also, without prayer, there can be no lasting celibacy."

It is clear that the prayer mentioned here is contemplative prayer, which permits us to direct our gaze in faith upon the Lord.

The necessity of contemplation today

But that is enough to show to what extent the contemplative dimension of the Christian faith is, today more than ever, necessary to the world. Further, the number of Christians called by God to receive a special charism of contemplation is no less now than it was in the past. And I am not talking here only of religious dedicated to contemplation nor of the contemplative life lived among men, which owes its origin to Father de Foucauld, but of lay persons, many of whom are immersed in activities in the world.[1]

[1] Here is one testimony among several others: "I am a social worker in a foundry. God in his grace has been so merciful to me that I have experienced what you say about contemplation. It is a genuine experience – and several people around me have had it in the thick of things – of the merciful presence of the Holy Spirit in the mind and the soul. Someone may come and tell me this is not so, that it is all imagination. I would reply: 'I see your face in front of me, I recognize it. I would be dishonest if I denied it. This is just as true of God who enters into communication with us when he chooses.' I repeat that around me several people have received these graces and these same people would lay down their lives rather than deny this."

Nevertheless, the conditions in which we live have seldom been less favourable to contemplative prayer, as Pope Paul VI recently reminded us in an address to the Cistercians:

"Today you are in the midst of a world that seems to be in the grip of a fever which finds its way even into the sanctuary and solitude. Noise and uproar have engulfed almost everything. Above all, people can no longer be recollected. At the mercy of a thousand distractions, they are in the habit of dissipating their energies upon modern culture in its many forms. Newspapers, magazines, books, flood the privacy of our home and our hearts. With up-to-date travel, contacts between peoples have become much more frequent than formerly. Journeys covering even long distances, reunions, group activities, and other such enterprises, are, now, everyday occurrences. This is not, of course, to deny or reject the true values of human progress. Yet it must be admitted that it is more difficult than formerly to find the opportunity for that recollection during which the soul can be wholly occupied with God."

Nevertheless, it is precisely in this kind of world that Providence, through the person of Father de Foucauld, inaugurated the birth and growth of a new kind of contemplative life of which something should be said.

A new kind of religious life

The contemplative vocation that originated with Brother Charles of Jesus and was put into practice by his Little Brothers in the form of a new kind of life in religion, affords an important witness to this evolution in the religious and contemplative life.

To be authentic, this evolution must be marked both by its fidelity to divine realities, without which it could not exist, and by a deepening of these same values through greater participation in the world.

Now, the kind of contemplation bequeathed to us by Father de Foucauld is characterized not simply by the fact that this life is lived in the world, sharing in the conditions of the poor – a fact which of itself entails a change in the way in which it is lived. At a deeper level, this life of contemplation, centred on the Heart of Christ, opens on to the mystery of charity towards men, contemplated at its divine source. This enables us to see, through the life of Brother Charles, the deep unity – and this is not the same thing as identity – that must exist between our love for Christ and our love for men. The entire life of Father de Foucauld is consecrated to the Heart of Christ, as the one point where – beyond, of course, man's earthly life – these two movements of love that seem so different in the conditions of their actual realization, converge. One movement leads us to love God to the point of separation from all created things; the other, to love men in a total participation in their everyday tasks on earth.

It is not my purpose to recount here the history of the birth and growth of this contemplative movement in the Church. I will stress, however, its most original features.

When Father de Foucauld decided to abandon the traditional framework of the cloister with the purpose of trying out a new way of life, he was impelled by an urge, that he found irresistible, not only to model himself on Jesus of Nazareth, but also to share in the everyday life of the poor. His vocation was marked, then, from its very beginning, by this twofold movement towards establishing a harmony, in the existential reality of his consecrated life, between the friendship that he wanted to show to men and his desire to belong wholly to Christ in contemplation.

It must be admitted that up to our own times the religious life, especially in its contemplative form, has been strongly marked in its spirituality, and in the practical application of this, by a demand for a radical separation from life in the world. It consequently assumed a kind of purely other-worldly character. This other-worldliness, which is conspicuous in the lives of the Carthusians, for example, affords an eloquent testimony of the absolute quality of man's gift to God: a testimony which remains valid and necessary in the Church today. Nevertheless, the inability to understand this kind of separation and the hostility to which it gives rise, continue to grow in proportion as Christians are becoming increasingly committed to complex and demanding tasks in the world.

Love for men in the Heart of Christ

The change in the contemplative life, which Father de Foucauld brought about in its early stages, and which took a more precise form in the Fraternities, has a bearing on the following points.

Inspired by the contemplation of Christ at Nazareth, the disciples of Father de Foucauld choose, as an essential element in their contemplative life in religion, participation in the work and living conditions of the poor. This involves their being almost wholly deprived of a minimum of silence, detachment, and time to give to prolonged prayer – generally considered privileged, if not indispensable, conditions for contemplation. Not, indeed, that the Brothers question the value of these. They feel an urgent need to revert to them at regular intervals, accentuating, if that be possible, their spiritual value. Moreover, these periods of respite are marked by the absolute quality of silence, solitude, and dispossession proper to the desert. It is also worth observing (this is by the way) that the young, today, are often more at ease in the setting of solitude and prayer stripped of all un-essentials, inspired by the Desert Fathers, than they are with the more complicated practices and spiritual exercises characteristic of congregations founded nearer our own times.

Between these periods of special solitude with God, the Little Brothers are required to express their life of union with Christ, and to find nourishment for it, not only in daily fidelity to prayer, but particularly in the dispossession demanded by a life of poverty and toil, as well as in friendship with their fellow men. Yet, in the case of the followers of Charles de Foucauld, this union with God, attained in everyday life through human relationships, must not be interpreted in the sense, too often advocated at the present time, which suggests that to encounter men in charity is, if not the only way of encountering God, the only authentic one. Every other attempt to encounter God or find union with him on the plane of prayer or in living a spiritual life is considered an illusion or, at best, the satisfaction of a legitimate psychological need for renewal through the refreshment afforded by the peace that comes from silence and meditation.

Yes, what we do to the least of our brothers we do for God, and no one can love God if he does not love his brother. So, then, love moves in one direction, but its objectives, nevertheless, are twofold, for God remains distinct from our brothers and deserves to be loved for himself. Christ lives in the hearts of men, but what I can find in my brothers is not God in person, nor Christ himself, but his likeness, his presence by grace, the

marvels of his love and his compassion, which are indeed
a wondrous object for our contemplation. Yet, if we are
content to search for God in loving our brothers and in
giving ourselves to them generously, do we not still remain
closed, as it were, within the limitations of humanity?
Are we, then, capable of contemplating only man – in
his mystery, indeed, but also in his limitations? Are we to
be reduced to contemplating the works of the Lord, without being able to contemplate the Lord himself? I would
venture to suggest that a Christian, no longer concerned
to contemplate the Lord and to love him above all else,
would no longer be able to love his fellow men as Jesus
loved them – no matter how dedicated he might be to
the service of others. It is only in the Heart of Christ that
we can be united to the source, in its fulness, of this loving
friendship which, having its origin in God, overflows
upon men – a friendship in which every Christian should
try steadfastly to share.

It is this reality, implanted in their hearts by contemplation, that the Little Brothers try to transmit and to
share with others, not only through their hidden union
with Jesus and their silent intercession, but particularly
by disposing themselves, through a life led in the midst
of men, to give others a practical evidence of this friendship. The fact of sharing in the ordinary day to day life
of the mass of human beings enables the Little Brothers
to reveal to these, under the sign of an authentic friendship, something of the reality of God's love. The life they
lead among men, and the friendship to which they give

witness, should be a living proof that contemplation of God, far from cutting us off from others, alone allows us to love them in the manner in which God loves them. The Brothers, by their lives, should testify that only in the Heart of Christ, who is both God and man – who adores the Father and loves man to the point of laying down his life for each one of us – can this union be realized: a union, otherwise unattainable, between created and non-created, the world and eternity. The Heart of Christ may be thought of as a point in infinity, at which two seemingly divergent or parallel lines meet: that of the world, which is God's creation entrusted to the labour of men – the image of which passes – and that of the eternal kingdom already initiated here on earth.[1]

[1] From this single root and its twofold stem was to emerge also the Fraternity of the Little Brothers of the Gospel. Indeed, the new aspect in this vocation to spread the Gospel is contained, in its entirety, in this twofold stem. The one root consists of a living faith, that flowers in a charism of contemplation of the Heart of Christ.

The first stem emerging from this contemplation constitutes a sharing in the ineffable act whereby Jesus contemplates his Father, as well as in the perpetual prayer of adoration and intercession which springs from it. The apostolate of a Little Brother of the Gospel will bear the mark of this contemplative root, to the point of being, first and foremost, the witness of a personal experience: "That which we have heard, that which our eyes have seen, that which has met our gaze . . . this we pass on to you." The reality of this intimacy with Jesus alone will permit the extreme simplicity of the language used by those who give testimony to what they have seen. Cut off from the root of contemplation, this simplicity would soon become barren, ineffectual words.

To the extent that Father de Foucauld and after him the Little Brothers have remained wholly centred on the Heart of Christ, they have been able to give themselves to men in friendship, in a true sense. This friendship had become for the Brothers something which they felt was demanded of them by their contemplation of the Sacred Heart, and which, furthermore, remained enfolded, as it were, in this Heart while they were giving it practical expression day by day in their work and in their contacts with others.

The contemplation of Christ, friend of men, should accustom us to look at others as Jesus looked at them – that is, in the perspective of their eternity. This all-

The second stem, that of the boundless friendship of God for men, contemplated in the Heart of Christ and revealed in his making his dwelling among men, will find expression in the life of the Little Brother of the Gospel, not only through the simplicity with which, following the example of Jesus, he will share the life of men, but by an apostolic approach which springs from this friendship, along with an attitude of understanding, respect, and patience which flows from it. Separated from its root, this stem, which constitutes friendship, will end as no more than a barren participation in the human condition and a weakening of the responsibility for spreading the Gospel message.

The whole religious and apostolic life of the Little Brothers takes its origin, then, from this single contemplative root and the development of this twofold stem, in the perspective of an invitation from Jesus and his Church to spread the Gospel among men. It must be stressed once more that, in the tradition of the vocation proper to the followers of Charles de Foucauld, these two stems cannot be separated either from their root or from each other, without their withering and consequently losing all strength and fruitfulness.

embracing look of love reaches into the void which is in each one of us and which only God can fill. There is a way of loving men which reveals them in all their mystery. To know and to love men in this way, far from turning us away from the contemplation of God, brings us back to it unfailingly. And so friendship for men fans the flame of contemplation the measure of which is love; provided, that is, we know how to guard against the illusions and deceptions of a friendship turned in upon itself or confined within the horizons of life on earth.

I have said that union with the Heart of Jesus is essential to the vocation of a Little Brother. Indeed, whatever one may think of this or that devotion to the Sacred Heart, it remains none the less true that the Heart of Christ corresponds to a reality that is human and divine, transcendent and lasting: the ultimate revelation of Love incarnate.

For a like reason the Eucharist is the focal point in the life of the Fraternities. This Sacrament, indeed, gives expression to, and communicates, the gift of this divine love both in the redemptive sacrifice offered to the Father and in the union with this same love shared among all. In the Eucharist every Brother should find the presence of God. It should be a sacred sign: one which he needs all the more because his life is in danger of being submerged in a milieu from which all trace of God is excluded. The Eucharist is a sign that continually reminds the Brothers to renew their vocation. Moreover, where all is materialism, in the midst of the noise and the

grime of cities, it is their cell and their cloister. Every day,
in this Sacrament, the Little Brothers unite themselves to
the sacrifice of Jesus and participate in the prayer of the
Son who does not cease to make intercession for men, in
the presence of the Father.

To be witnesses of Christ

A life of this kind, by reason of the spirituality which inspires it, the manner in which it is lived, the means which it employs, is surely within the reach, at least to some extent, of all Christians. Moreover it shows that a union of this kind with God, the seed of which is already present in the gifts conferred by the Holy Spirit in Baptism, needs only to come to full growth – in our times no less than formerly – in all those who love the Lord and want to bear him witness in this world. It is an urgent invitation – in a world in which the spiritual side of man is stunted – to work that this seed of contemplation may come to fulness in proportion to our temporal or apostolic commitments. For if the Christian vocation, to be perfect, calls for just such a contemplative dimension, what about the life dedicated to the apostolate? Does it not by its very nature require of those who are witnesses of Christ and his message that they should have known him through personal experience of God in contemplation, before testifying to him through word of mouth? There is no need to stress that perhaps it is only on this condition that the apostolate will remain authentic, in view of the complex methods and organisations to which it is tempted, or obliged, to resort in an effort to be effective.

Perhaps I ought to recall at this point to what extent the role of the contemplative is vital to the Church. Of course, the grace of contemplation extends beyond the limits of the cloister and of those religious Orders who make it their specific end. In this sphere there prevails all the unpredictable freedom of choice that is proper to love – on the part of God who makes the first advances and likewise on the part of those who respond. To appreciate this, one has only to look into the hearts of those men and women who have been consumed with the love of God. Here, we are face to face with a hidden life in which a mysterious dialogue takes place between infinite Being, Truth, and Love, and his creature. For every mind that is ready to understand it, this fact remains an irrefutable sign that there is a personal God who truly loves man and draws him to himself as to his final end.

Renewal, but from within

The contemplative Orders are there not only to offer, to those who have been called, the conditions most conducive to a life of prayer, but also to be in the Church a collective sign, for all to see, of this intimate relationship with God. I shall not dwell on the mission of adoration and intercession on behalf of men to which contemplatives are called. No one would question this, and it has been reaffirmed by the Church time and again, especially during the last Council.

However, many men and women in the religious life feel that their vocation as contemplatives has been undermined. I am not speaking here of personal difficulties involving psychological adjustment, for these do not put into question the value of contemplation as such; they relate only to means or methods of formation which no one denies should be thought out afresh. I want rather to speak of a tendency, among religious living as contemplatives, to justify, in the eyes of the world and in their own, a form of the monastic or religious life which is questioned. No longer really believing in the life to which they are committed, they devote themselves to temporal or apostolic activities beneficial to mankind. Nonetheless, the unease remains. For why keep up an appearance if one no longer believes in the reality?

The renewal, so desirable not only in the monastic but in the religious life in all its forms – none of which can ever, in fact, dispense with the contemplative dimension – presupposes, above all, that one faces realistically the end in view: namely, to form religious to a life of prayer. Now, it is not possible to renew means, rules, or methods, unless there is established beforehand a basis of clear, well-founded convictions as to the nature and value of prayer. Also necessary is a heartfelt desire to put oneself in readiness to receive the genuine grace of contemplation which God alone can bestow.

Only on these conditions will life in religion be fully authentic. The young have a horror, and rightly so, of what they describe as "artificial". This adjective is often used to qualify any kind of religious observance or practice. There is some justification for such a reaction. An attitude or way of behaviour which does not correspond to a reality or is not conducive to lead to it or to give it expression, can, indeed, be described as "artificial". This state of things can result from a failure to adjust means to ends. The means, then, must be renewed. And this brings us to a psychological problem, calling for the use of common sense. But the feeling that something is "artificial" can also come – and this is vastly more serious – from the fact that observances have no longer any meaning, because the realities on which the religious life rests are, when it comes to putting them into practice, subject to doubt.

The life of a monk consecrated to prayer, in solitude and silence, is not artificial if the invisible world, towards which his entire life is directed, is, in fact, real; if an intimate relationship with God is possible; if Christ, the Blessed Virgin, saints, and angels constitute a living world with which man can enter into communication through the grace of Christ. If this is so, there is nothing artificial about the liturgical cycle, silence, meditation, periods of time devoted to prayer, union with the cross of Jesus, and a life of brotherhood lived in community. On the other hand, if this invisible world is not what the simple faith of the Church and the saints have declared it to be; if no true communication with this invisible world is possible; if the one worth-while task for men must be to work for the construction of the earthly city, then, certainly, not only the monastic, but every form of consecrated life is artificial, except in so far as it is reduced to a more concentrated way of living in brotherhood, in the service of our fellow men – which is not without value, but is, nevertheless, quite another matter.

Between the consecrated contemplative and religious life as it has always been lived in the Church, and to which countless saints have given witness – between this and certain theological views which amount almost to its denial, we have to choose. And I do not intend to go back on what I have said at the beginning about the premises concerning contemplation.

RENEWAL, BUT FROM WITHIN   77

The young have a passion for authenticity and this demand is a healthy one. Yes, we should certainly look for authenticity and truth, even if it means going against certain popular trends. All is not the work of the Holy Spirit, in the general upheaval to which Christianity is at present exposed. "Discernment of spirits" is more than ever necessary. Is truth, one asks, to be found in every whim of man? Or, on the contrary, must not man allow himself to be moulded and led by the truth that comes to him from God, even though it may mean being stripped of all things in obedience to the cross? Here, too, we have to choose.

I am convinced that renewal in the religious life, particularly in that of contemplation, demands a courageous authenticity on our part, one which must be measured by the truth of Christ and the faith. Far from watering down the essential values of silence and solitude with God, we should assert these in their stark simplicity. I have said how well the young, called by God, respond to these values: how, even if they grope their way slowly, they prefer to go straight to their goal in the simplicity of the Gospel and in poverty.

Finally, as Thomas Merton has done well to stress, the opening of the monasteries on to the world must not result in a vague watering down of the demands of contemplation, under the pretext of being informed about everything – this can often be only a psychological compensation for a detachment that goes against the grain. Rather, it should mean becoming capable of sharing the blessing of contemplation – without loss to this – with those who desire it : for this is the proper role of religious living a contemplative life. No one can do everything. The world today, whatever one may think, will have more and more need of these oases of silence and with-drawal for prayer. And this presupposes that religious will be both totally faithful to their vocation as contem-platives, and will find the means – and these are of all kinds – to extend a welcome not just to any passer-by or someone who comes merely out of curiosity, but to all who sincerely desire to pause for prayer and silence.

Yes, I have faith in the future of a religious life thus renewed. Civilization, whatever form it may take, will never succeed in stifling that nostalgia at the heart of man – that longing which only God will satisfy. The adjustments necessary in the religious life, or rather the renewal, will not take place on the level of material modifications which are purely exterior; nor again by cutting down the time given to prayer, so as to satisfy some passing whim or some psychological need. Renewal will come from within, through thinking out afresh the basic and permanent values which constitute this same life when lived in the full light of faith.

I not only have confidence in the future of a religious life renewed in this way. In an age in which man is per-sistently and brutally confronted with his destiny, I am convinced the contemplative life is called upon to be diffused more and more throughout Christianity. There are circumstances in which the Christian can find himself cornered: he feels he must either become a contemplative or cease being a Christian. Just as with Saint Ignatius, as I have said, the religious life infiltrated apostolic activities, so today we are, I believe, at a stage in the evolution of the Church, which will take the form of a more deliberate and more universal diffusion of contemplation throughout the entire Christian society.